CONTENTS

4

TRADITION

Lyrics by
SHELDON HARNICK

Music by
JERRY BOCK
Arranged by ROBERT SCHULTZ

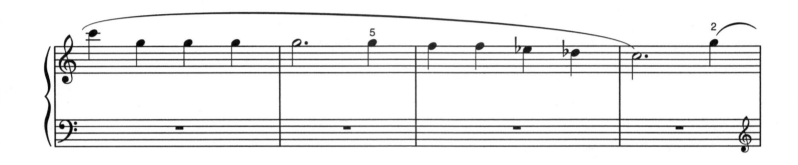

Tradition - 8 - 1
AS006

TRADITION
Jewish Music

Arranged & Edited by
Robert Schultz

Editor: ROBERT SCHULTZ
Project Manager: TONY ESPOSITO
Production Coordinator: ZOBY PEREZ
Book Illustration & Design: JORGE PAREDES

CONTENTS

6

10

Tradition - 8 - 7

Dai - dai - dai - dai,   dai - dai - dai - dai,   dai - dai - dai - dai,   dai - dai - dai - dai - dai.

Dai - dai - dai - dai,   dai - dai - dai - dai,   dai - dai - dai - dai,   dai - dai - dai - dai - dai.

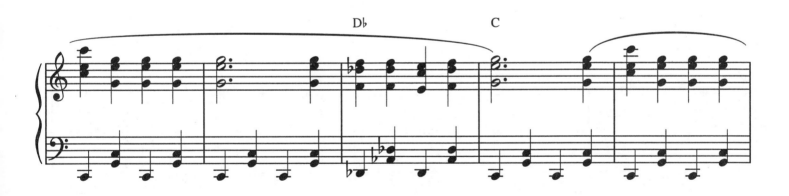

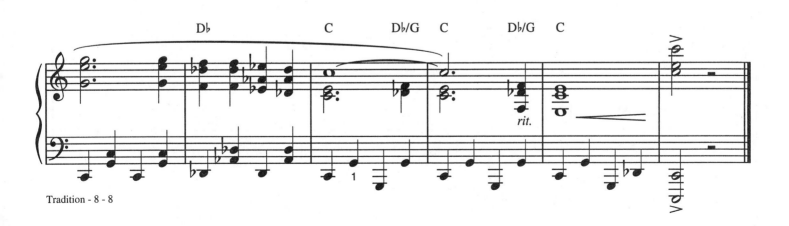

Tradition - 8 - 8

From the Broadway Musical "FIDDLER ON THE ROOF"

MATCHMAKER

Lyrics by
SHELDON HARNICK

Music by
JERRY BOCK
Arranged by ROBERT SCHULTZ

Bright waltz

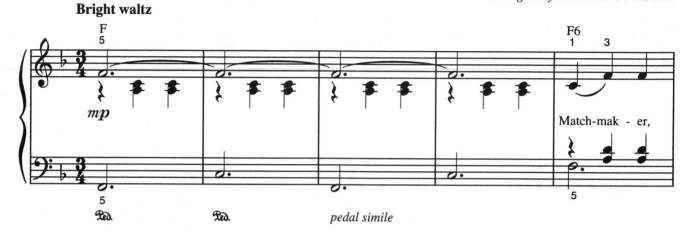

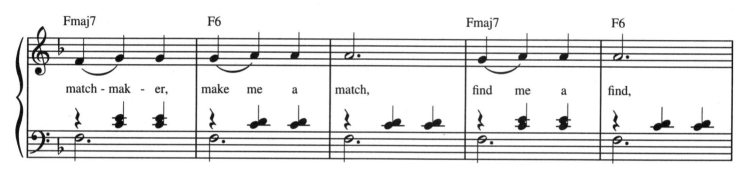

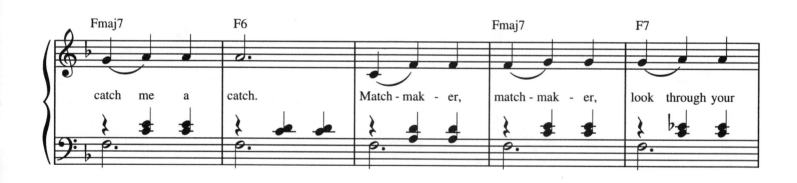

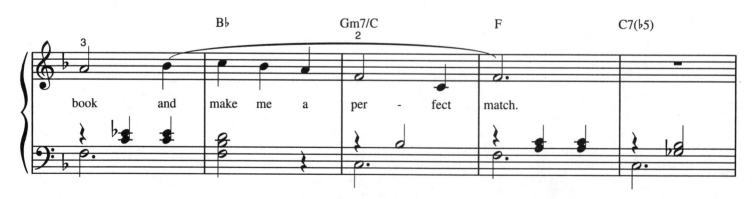

Matchmaker - 3 - 1
AS006

From the Broadway Musical "FIDDLER ON THE ROOF"

SABBATH PRAYER

Lyrics by
SHELDON HARNICK

Music by
JERRY BOCK
Arranged by ROBERT SCHULTZ

Sabbath Prayer - 3 - 1
AS006

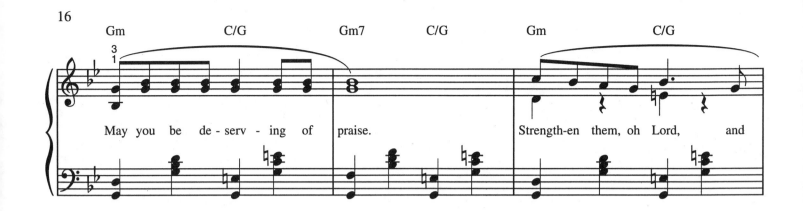

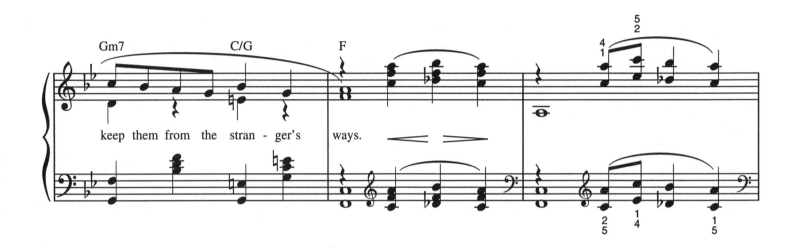

wives.
May He send you hus-bands who will care for you. May the Lord pro-tect and de-

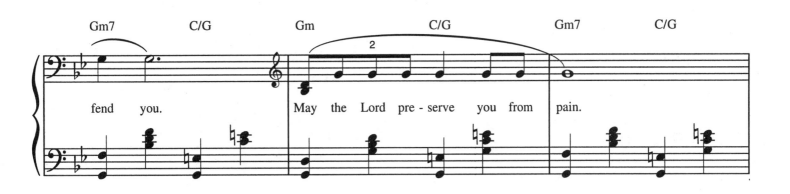

fend you. May the Lord pre-serve you from pain.

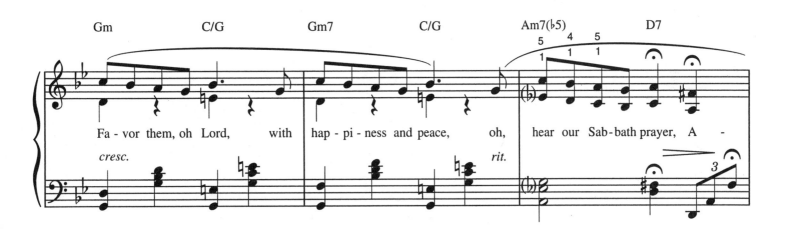

Fa-vor them, oh Lord, with hap-pi-ness and peace, oh, hear our Sab-bath prayer, A-

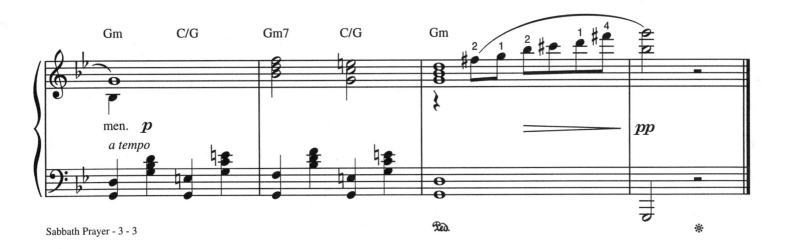

men.

From the Broadway Musical "FIDDLER ON THE ROOF"

SUNRISE, SUNSET

Lyrics by
SHELDON HARNICK

Music by
JERRY BOCK
Arranged by ROBERT SCHULTZ

Sunrise, Sunset - 4 - 1
AS006

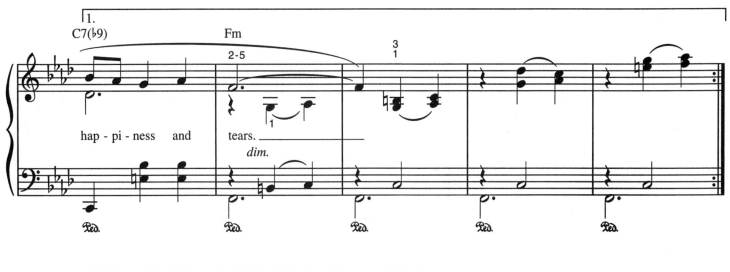

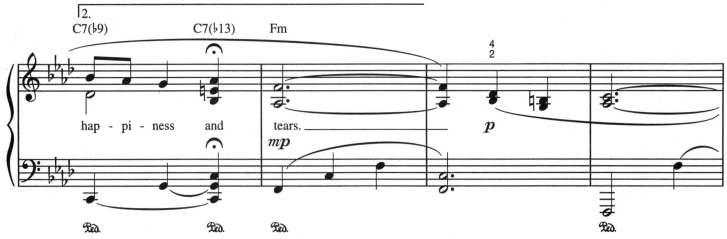

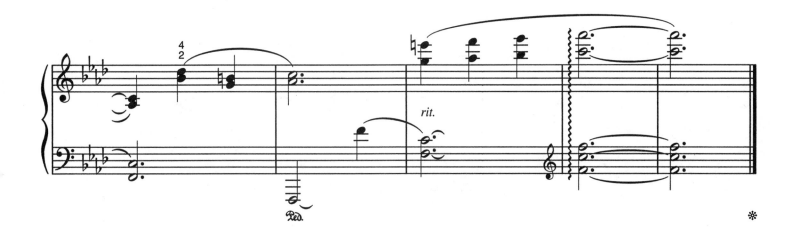

Verse 2:
What words of wisdom can I give them?
How can I help to ease their way?
Now they must learn from one another,
Day by day.
They look so natural together,
Just like two newlyweds should be.
Is there a canopy in store for me?
(To Chorus:)

From the Broadway Musical "FIDDLER ON THE ROOF"

TO LIFE

Lyrics by
SHELDON HARNICK

Music by
JERRY BOCK
Arranged by ROBERT SCHULTZ

With spirit

To Life - 5 - 1
AS006

Verse 2:
To Lazar Wolfe. To Tevye.
To Tzeitel, your daughter. My wife.
May all your futures be pleasant ones,
Not like our present ones.
Drink, L'chaim,
To life, to life, L'chaim,
L'chaim, L'chaim, to life.
It takes a wedding to make us say:
Let's live another day.
Drink, L'chaim, to life.

We'll raise a glass and sip a drop of schnapps
In honor of the great, good luck that favored you.
We know that when good fortune favors two such men,
It stands to reason we deserve it too.

To us and our good fortune!
Be happy. Be healthy. Long life!
And if our good fortune never comes,
Here's to whatever comes.
Drink, L'chaim, to life!
(to 2nd ending)

HEVENU SHALOM ALECHEM

TRADITIONAL
Arranged by ROBERT SCHULTZ

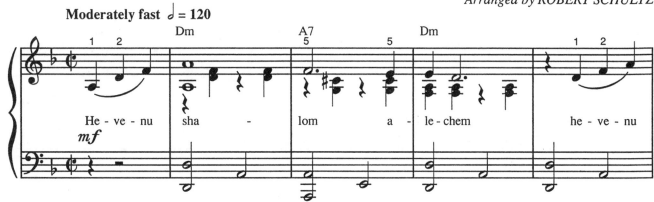

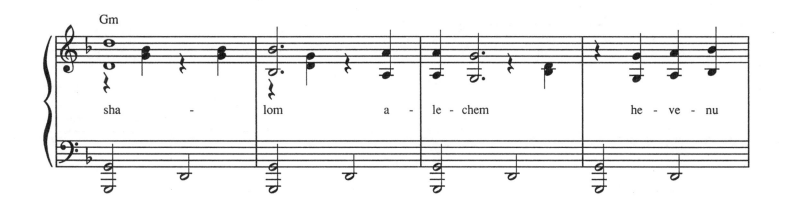

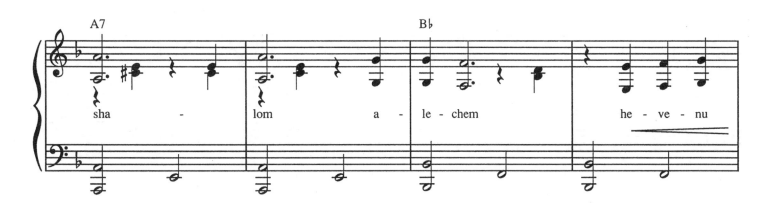

ARTZA ALINU

TRADITIONAL
Arranged by ROBERT SCHULTZ

Artza Alinu - 2 - 1

We are ascending, our way we're wending to Israel's ancient land.
We are ascending, our way we're wending to Israel's ancient land.
We've done our plowing, finished our sowing,
Worked with the harrow, ended our hoeing;
But, though we've sown with sadness, we've not yet reaped with gladness.
But, though we've sown with sadness, we've not yet reaped with gladness.

BASHANA HABA'A

N. HIRSH
Arranged by ROBERT SCHULTZ

BEI MIR BIST DU SCHON
(Means That You're Grand)

Original Lyrics by JACOB JACOBS
English Version by
SAMMY CAHN and SAUL CHAPLIN

Music by
SHOLOM SECUNDA
Arranged by ROBERT SCHULTZ

Bei Mir Bist Du Schon - 2 - 1
AS006

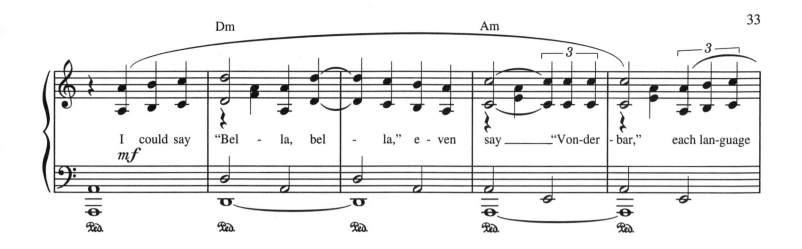

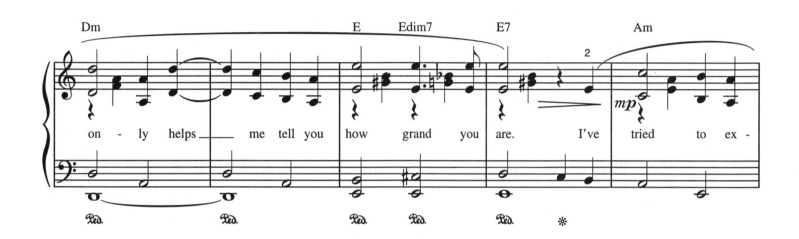

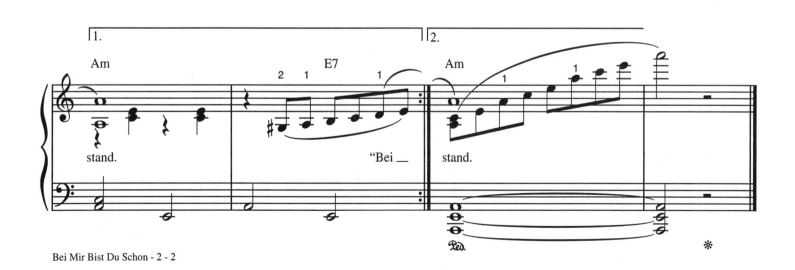

Bei Mir Bist Du Schon - 2 - 2

HATIKVA

ISRAELI NATIONAL ANTHEM
Arranged by ROBERT SCHULTZ

Hatikva - 2 - 1

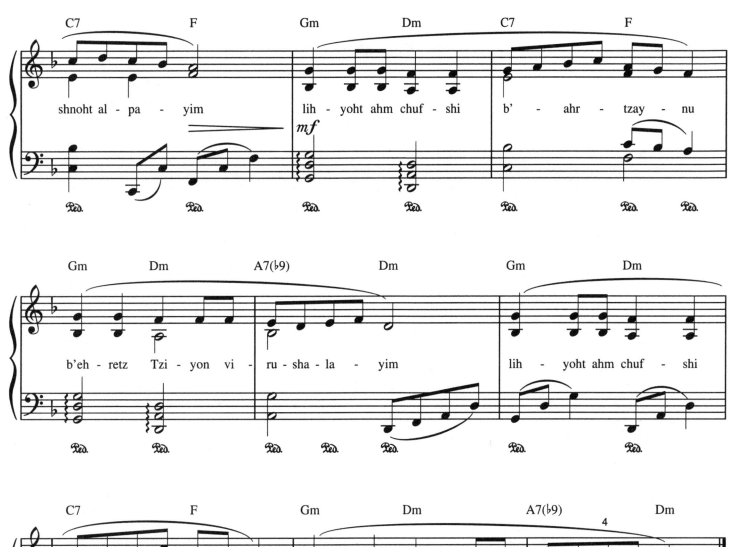

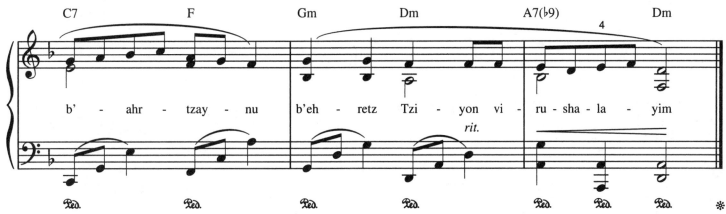

So long as the heart of the Jew beats
And his eye is turned to the East,
So long does our ancient hope
Of returning to Zion still live.

HAVA NAGILA

HASSIDIC
Arranged by ROBERT SCHULTZ

JERUSALEM OF GOLD

N. SHEMER
Arranged by ROBERT SCHULTZ

OIF'N PRIPITCHIK

TRADITIONAL
Arranged by ROBERT SCHULTZ

Oif'n Pripitchik - 2 - 1

By the fireside, where the embers glow, through the wintry days,
There the teacher, softly, with the little ones, chants the alef beys. (repeat)
So, you little ones, learn these lessons well, letters of God's law;
Sing them once again, and now then, once again: kometz alef aw. (repeat)

OSE SHALOM

N. HIRSH
Arranged by ROBERT SCHULTZ

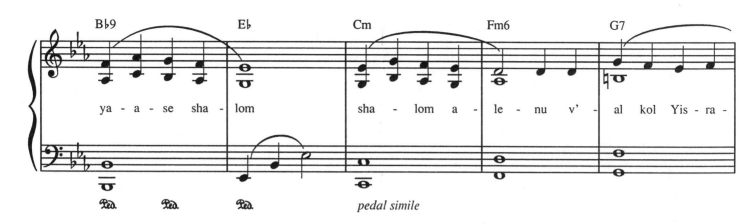

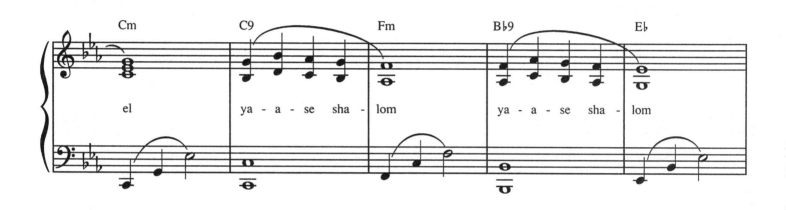

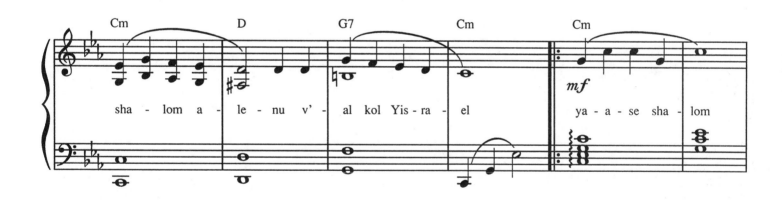

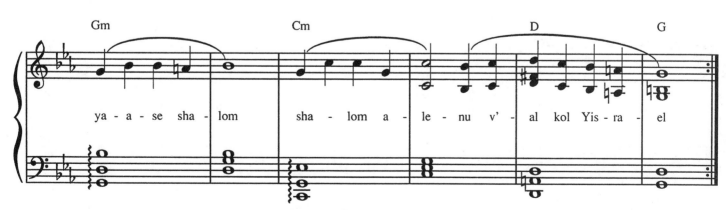

Ose Shalom - 3 - 2

44

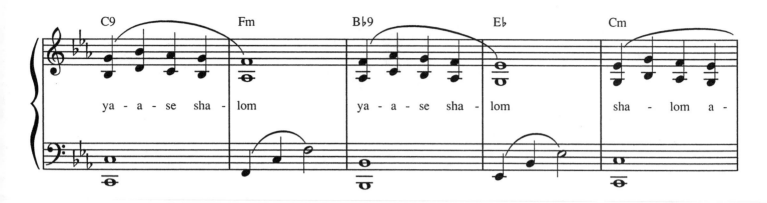

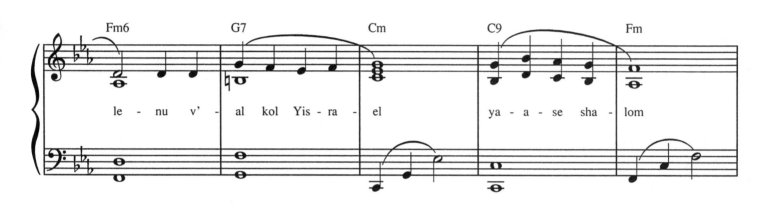

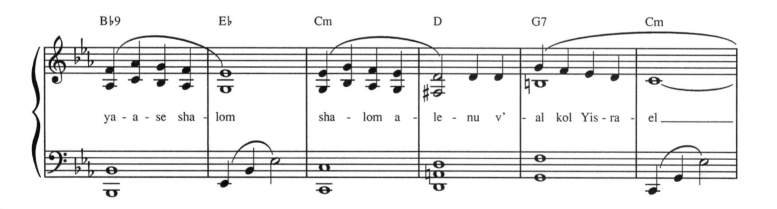

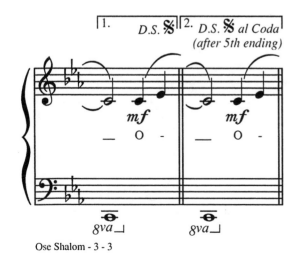

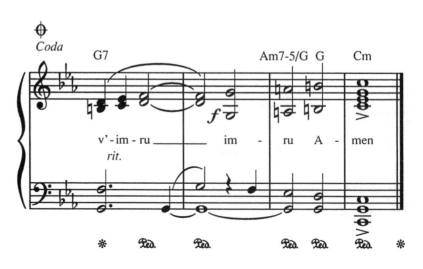

Ose Shalom - 3 - 3

ZUM GALI GALI

TRADITIONAL
Arranged by ROBERT SCHULTZ

Fast, with spirit

SIMAN TOV

TRADITIONAL
Arranged by ROBERT SCHULTZ

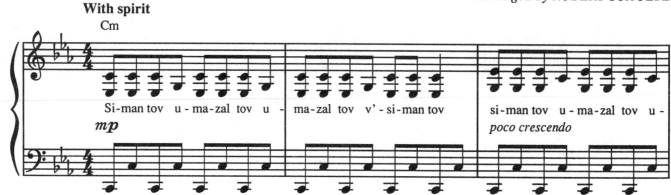

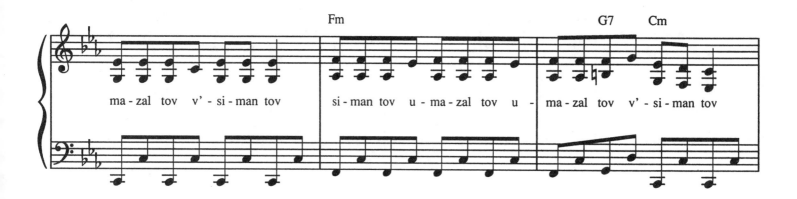

Siman Tov - 2 - 1

TZENA TZENA

I. MIRON and J. GROSSMAN
Arranged by ROBERT SCHULTZ

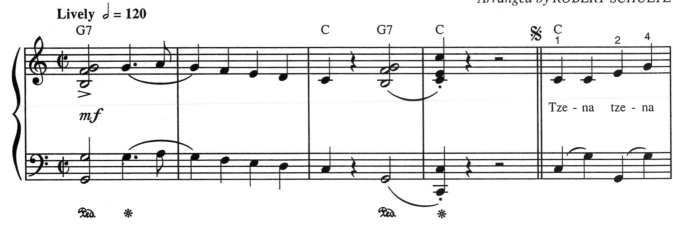

Tzena Tzena - 2 - 1

LET'S BE FRIENDS

TRADITIONAL
Arranged by ROBERT SCHULTZ

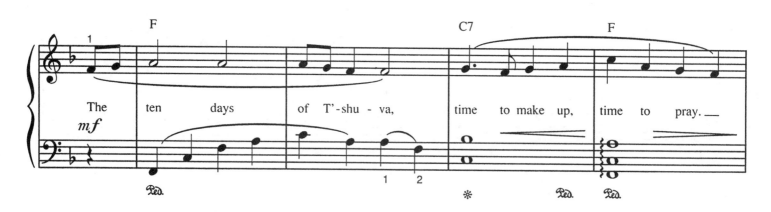

L'SHANA TOVA

TRADITIONAL
Arranged by ROBERT SCHULTZ

May you be inscribed for a good year.

TAPUCHIM UD'VASH

TRADITIONAL
Arranged by ROBERT SCHULTZ

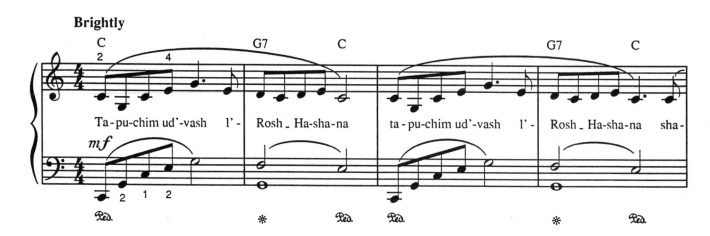

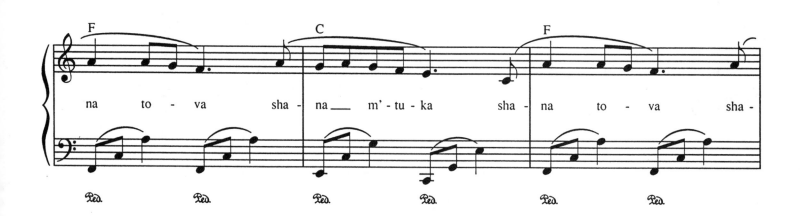

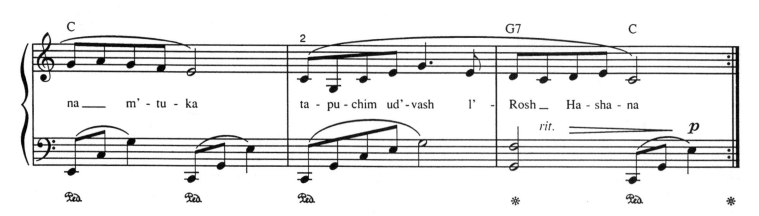

Apples dipped in honey for Rosh Hashana,
Apples dipped in honey for Rosh Hashana;
A good new year, a sweet new year,
A good new year, a sweet new year;
Apples dipped in honey for Rosh Hashana.

CHANUKAH

TRADITIONAL
Arranged by ROBERT SCHULTZ

Chanukah Chanukah, joyous holiday,
Candle light burning bright, helps to celebrate.
Chanukah Chanukah, dreydls spin and turn,
Spin and turn, spin and turn, while the candles burn.

BARUCH SHEL CHANUKAH

TRADITIONAL
Arranged by ROBERT SCHULTZ

55

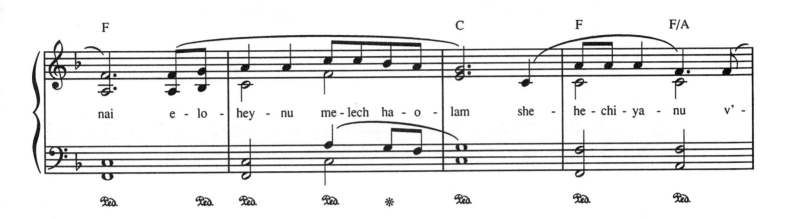

nai   e - lo - hey - nu   me - lech ha - o - lam   she - he - chi - ya - nu   v' -

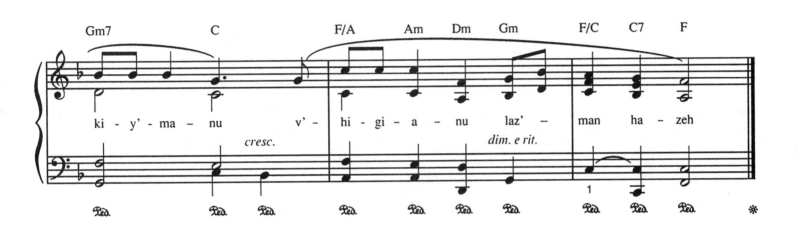

ki - y' - ma - nu   v' - hi - gi - a - nu   laz' - man   ha - zeh

cresc.   *dim. e rit.*

Blessed art Thou, O Lord, who hast commanded us
To kindle the Chanukah lights.
Blessed art Thou, who hast wrought miracles
For our fathers in those days.
Blessed art Thou, who hast brought us
Unto this season.

Baruch Shel Chanukah - 2 - 2

HANEROT HALALU

TRADITIONAL FOLK SONG
Arranged by ROBERT SCHULTZ

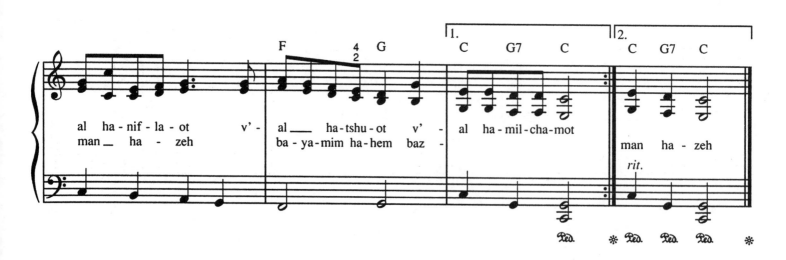

We kindle these lights for the wonders and the redemptions
Thou didst perform for our fathers through Thy holy priests.
These Chanukah lights are holy, and through them we sanctify Thy name.

I HAVE A LITTLE DREYDL

S.E. GOLDFARB
Arranged by ROBERT SCHULTZ

Verse 2:
It has a lovely body,
With leg so short and thin
And when it is all tired,
It drops and then I win.
(To Chorus:)

Verse 3:
My dreydl's always playful,
It loves to dance and spin;
A happy game of dreydl,
Come play, now, let's begin.
(To Chorus:)

LICHVOD HACHANUKAH

TRADITIONAL FOLK SONG
Arranged by ROBERT SCHULTZ

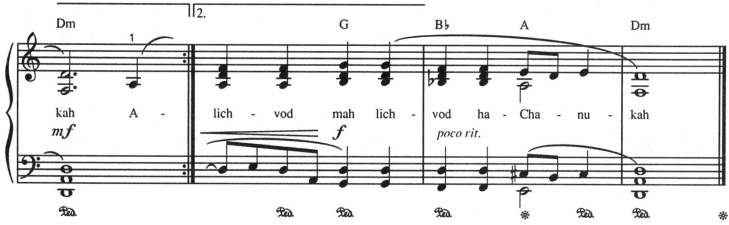

Verse 1:	Verse 1:
I-mi nat-na le-vi-vah li	*My mother baked me a levivah,*
Le-vi-vah cha-mah u-me-tu-ka	*A crisp and brown levivah,*
Le-vi-vah cha-mah u-me-tu-ka	*A crisp and brown levivah.*
Yod'im atem lich-vod mah	*Oh do you know what it's for?*
Yod'im atem lich-vod mah	*Oh do you know what it's for?*
Yod'im atem lich-vod mah	*Oh do you know what it's for?*
Lich-vod ha-Chanukah	*It's in honor of Chanukah.*

Verse 2:	Verse 2:
A-vi hid-lik nerot li	*My father lit the candles high,*
Ve-sha-mash lo a-vou-kah	*With the shammash' fiery light,*
Ve-sha-mash lo a-vou-kah	*With the shammash' fiery light.*
Yod'im atem lich-vod mah	*Oh do you know what it's for?*
Yod'im atem lich-vod mah	*Oh do you know what it's for?*
Yod'im atem lich-vod mah	*Oh do you know what it's for?*
Lich-vod ha-Chanukah	*It's in honor of Chanukah.*

MAOZ TZUR

(Rock of Ages)

TRADITIONAL
Arranged by ROBERT SCHULTZ

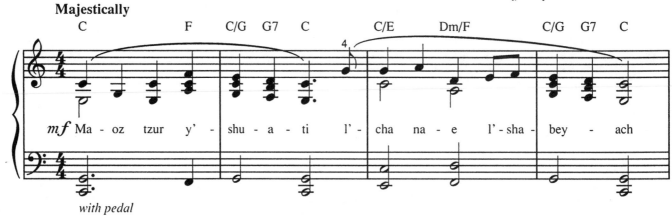

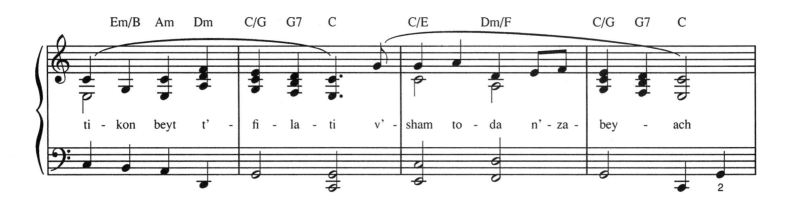

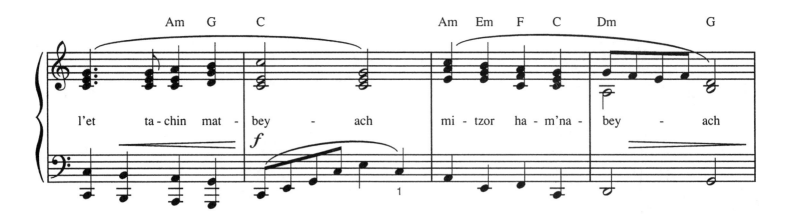

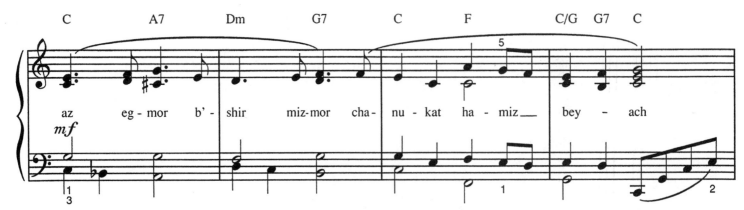

Maoz Tzur - 2 - 1

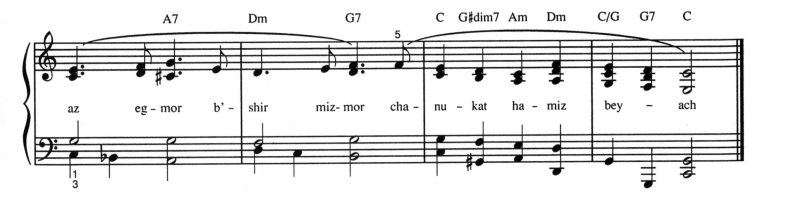

az eg – mor b' – shir miz – mor cha – nu – kat ha – miz bey – ach

Rock of ages, let our song
Praise Thy saving power;
Thou, amidst the raging foes,
Wast our shelt'ring tower.
Furious, they assailed us,
But Thine arm availed us,
And Thy word broke their sword
When our own strength failed us.

S'VIVON

Words by L. KIPNIS
TRADITIONAL FOLK SONG
Arranged by ROBERT SCHULTZ

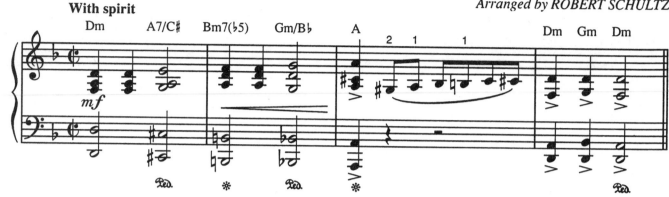

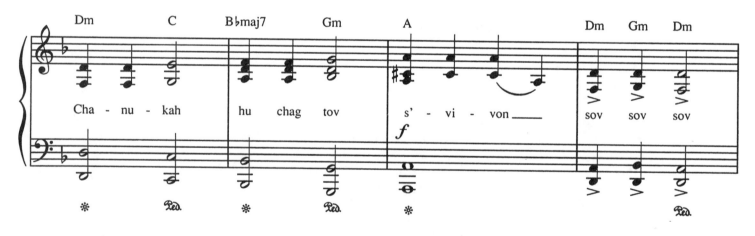

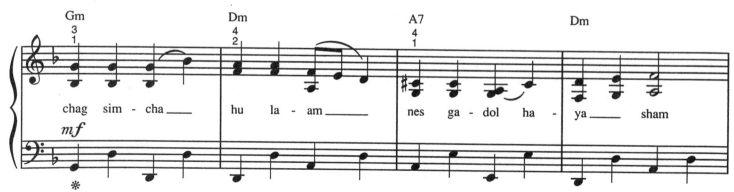

nes ga - dol ha - ya____ sham____ chag sim - cha____ hu la - am

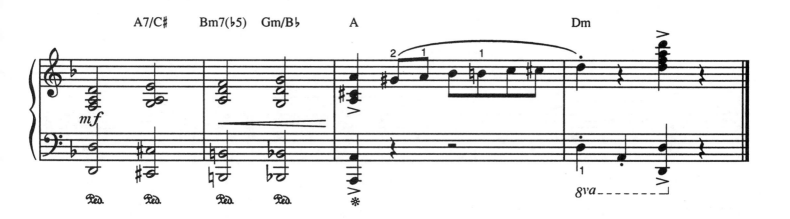

Little dreydl, spin and turn,
On Chanukah when candles burn;
On Chanukah when candles burn;
Little dreydl, spin and turn.
Celebrate with song and prayer,
A wondrous miracle happened there;
A wondrous miracle happened there,
Celebrate with song and prayer.

Y'MEY HACHANUKAH

Words by A. EVRONIN
TRADITIONAL FOLK SONG
Arranged by ROBERT SCHULTZ

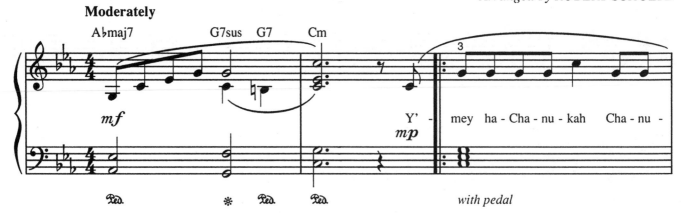

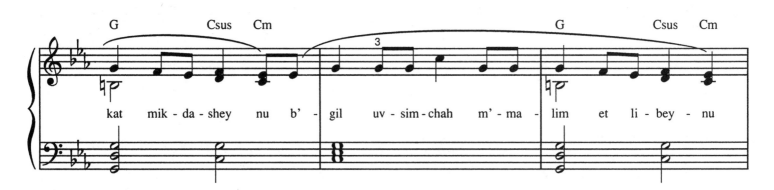

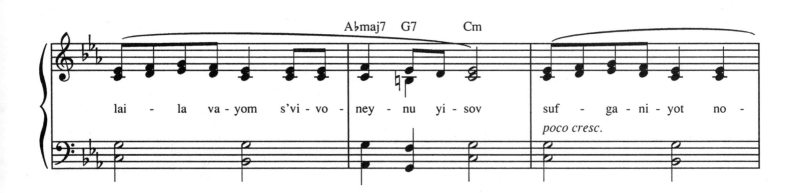

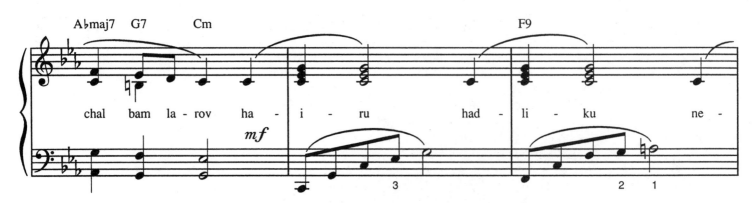

Y'mey Hachanukah - 2 - 1

Oh Chanukah, oh Chanukah, come light the menorah;
Let's have a party, we'll all dance the horah.
Gather 'round the table, we'll give you a treat;
Dreydls to play with and latkes to eat.
And while we are playing, the candles are burning low;
One for each night, they shed a sweet light to remind us of days long ago;
One for each night, they shed a sweet light to remind us of days long ago.

MY CANDLES

HASSIDIC
Arranged by ROBERT SCHULTZ

*Sing the correct number on each of the nights of Chanukah.

CHAG PURIM

TRADITIONAL
Arranged by ROBERT SCHULTZ

CHAD GADYA

TRADITIONAL
Arranged by ROBERT SCHULTZ

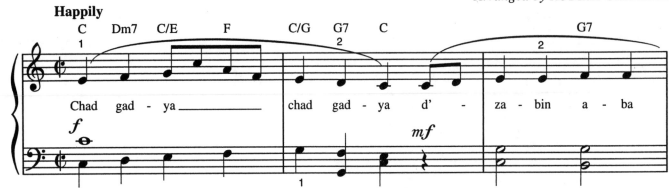

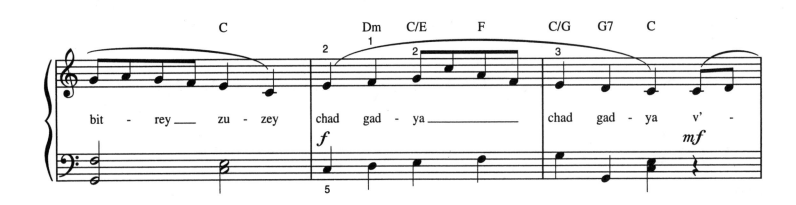

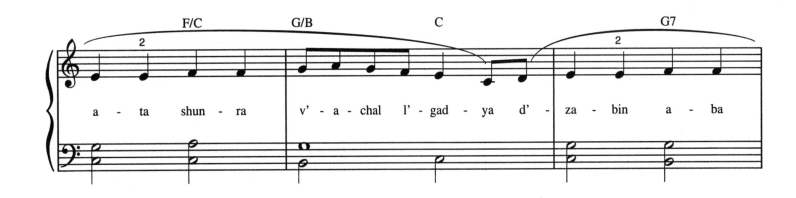

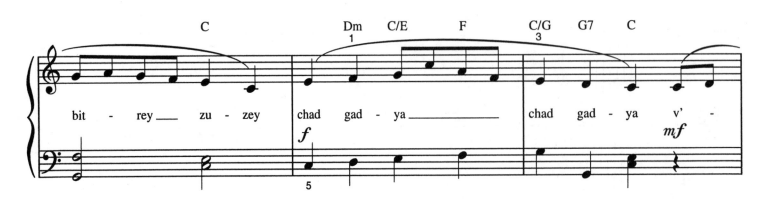

Chad Gadya - 2 - 1

DAYENU

TRADITIONAL FOLK SONG
Arranged by ROBERT SCHULTZ

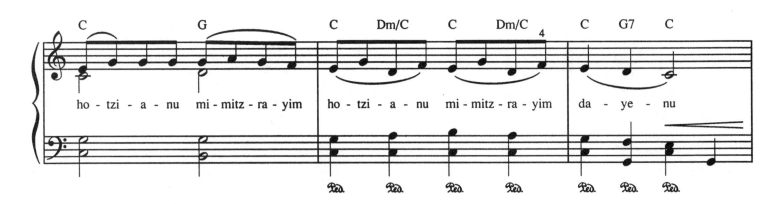

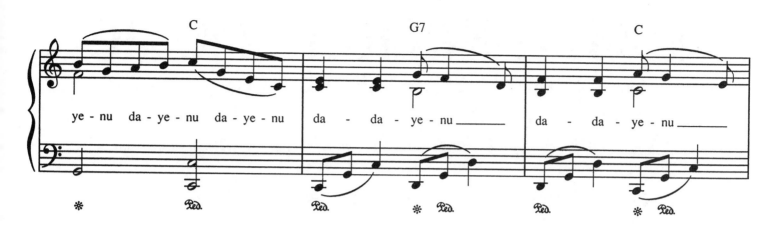

Verse 1:
I-lu ho-tzi ho-tzi-a-nu
ho-tzi-a-nu mi-mitz-ra-yim
ho-tzi-a-nu mi-mitz-ra-yim da-ye-nu

Refrain:
Da-da-ye-nu

Verse 2:
I-lu na-tan na-tan la-nu
Na-tan la-nu et ha-sha-bat
Na-tan la-nu et ha-sha-bat da-ye-nu
(Refrain:)

Verse 3:
I-lu na-tan na-tan la-nu
Na-tan la-nu et ha-to-rah
Na-tan la-nu et ha-to-rah da-ye-nu
(Refrain:)

Verse 1:
Had He led us out of Egypt,
Only led us out of Egypt,
Had He led us out of Egypt, dayenu.

Refrain:
Da-dayenu...

Verse 2:
Had He given us the Sabbath,
Only given us the Sabbath,
Had He given us the Sabbath, dayenu.
(Refrain:)

Verse 3:
Had He given us the Torah,
Only given us the Torah,
Had He given us the Torah, dayenu.
(Refrain:)

JEWISH HOLIDAY MUSIC
from the Schultz Piano Library
Superb piano arrangements, written and edited by Robert Schultz,
for pianists at every level, from beginner to professional

Editions for Beginners (Elementary/5 Finger)

(F3229PFX) FUN WITH 5 FINGER JEWISH HOLIDAY SONGS
18 traditional songs organized by holiday — High Holy Days, Chanukah, Purim, Passover and Songs of Israel; keyboard diagrams, lyrics, 32 pages.

(F3242PFX) COLOR ME CHANUKAH
9 standard Chanukah songs, children's favorites, with a coloring page for each song; crayons included, keyboard diagrams, lyrics, 32 pages.

Editions for Early Intermediate Students (Very Easy/Big Note)

(AF9544) ENJOY BIG NOTE JEWISH HOLIDAY SONGS
20 traditional songs organized by holiday — High Holy Days, Chanukah, Purim, Passover and Songs of Israel; lyrics, 36 pages.

(F3433P3X) ENJOY BIG NOTE CHANUKAH
9 standard Chanukah songs in order of difficulty; lyrics, 20 pages.

(AF9804) TRADITION
33 traditional and popular songs for holidays, weddings and all occasions, including selections from *Fiddler on the Roof*; lyrics, 76 pages.

Editions for Intermediate - Advanced Pianists

(F3319P2X) JEWISH HOLIDAY SONG CLASSICS (Easy Piano)
22 traditional songs organized by holiday — High Holy Days, Chanukah, Purim, Passover and Songs of Israel; lyrics, chord names, 40 pages.

(MF9641) JEWISH HOLIDAY SONG CLASSICS (Piano/Vocal/Chords)
Matches the easy piano edition with 3-stave arrangements; lyrics, chord names, 48 pages.

(PA02530) KOL NIDREI, Op. 47
Max Bruch's powerful and moving work for cello and orchestra, transcribed for concert pianists by Robert Schultz.

(AF9803) TRADITION
Intermediate Edition — 32 traditional and popular songs for holidays, weddings and all occasions, including selections from *Fiddler on the Roof*; lyrics, chord names, 72 pages.